Climate Change

A Selected Poetry Collection

2000—2017

by

Mahyar Mazloumi

deebeebooks.com
ISBN-13: 9781896794211

When I'm done writing,

Scrap paper remains for me,
And a unique poem for you.

*T*here's no place to hide.

I'm a desert,

And your steps break my silence.

One moment is sufficient

To return to life,

Through your eyes.

Jesus is impotent.

A cocoon

Was our ancient homeland,

And turning into butterflies,

Was our tradition.

Your warps and wefts will be ripped,

By suppressed happiness

Of expectant flowers.

Meaningless,

Vague,

Words!

My mind has adopted a vow of silence.

I wish you didn't take

My feelings away.

Your hands

Were flames.

I put my tired

Cold soul

Into the warmth of your hands,

To rise,

And then to die

With your gaze,

Again.

*T*he seconds

Are silent,

Longing for me

To write you.

I stare at you,

Wordless.

I don't know how to write

In your presence.

I was shattered

By your gaze

Into pieces.

Then reconstructed

By your kisses.

What a childish game!

Why did you grow up suddenly?

You will die

In a hospital,

While the instruments record

Your life signs.

You will die

Like a Neanderthal

In a cave.

What a strange story:

My empty mind,

And dotted-line thoughts;

A void paper,

And the trace of a sensual pencil;

My desire,

And the denial of the words.

What a strange story:

My arms,

And your embrace.

*D*aylight,

I think,

Is an excuse

For rays

To play with your shadow,

And for me

To get warm.

I hear a sound,

A repetitive hallucination.

Is it the night,

Waiting

To steal the flowers,

To dry out the rivers,

And to take your shadow away?

I cling to your shadow tightly.

I promised poetry,

To bring my words,

Sit on the front stairs,

Sharpen my pencil,

And write too many lies.

Then everybody throws

My poetry book in the fire.

Finally it is just you,

And me,

And a truthful silence.

I had a dream!

A bird nested

In your hands,

And flowers grew

Out of your shoulders.

The sky smiled

At you,

And the rain

Called your name.

I was in a meadow,

I guess,

When you called me,

Where your kisses

Were sunshine.

When I woke up,

My lips were still warm.

*I*n a garden,

You collected dew

For the flowers,

And made whirligigs

For the wind.

I looked for you,

In the crowded streets

Where it feels numb

In the afternoon

And sleepy at night.

When I arrived at the garden,

It was raining.

You were rain,

And I, wind.

Our bodies entangled,

And leaves

Swirled back

To the branches,

Green.

It howled,

When I held you

On the pavement

Under the leaves,

Among the hair of the street-girls,

And over the breasts

Of a naked woman,

In front of an open window.

Somebody shouted.

The window shut,

And the sound of us

Pouring against the window

Kept the man next door awake.

I'm jealous of all the men

Who loved you,

With their impotent gazes

And cold hands

Waiting for your warm touch.

I'm jealous of the wind

Blowing through your hair,

Mad and merry.

I'm jealous of the earth

Counting your steps

Eagerly.

This,

Before your eyes,

Seduced me.

Now I think they're right.

Wild storms

Removed the eternity

Of your kisses

From the meadow

That our bodies cuddled.

And our souls

Watched the sunset excitedly.

We were free,

We werc a silent eternity,

We could fit in dew drops

Under the evergreen trees.

Your kisses for me,

And your lips for

Whoever holds you in his arms.

$\mathcal{R}$epetition is boring,

Similar to

Having sex repeatedly.

Your scream resonates

Through the complexity of time,

Similar to

Returning to virginity

At the dawn of,

A sacred prostitution.

Such is the beginning

Of thoughts

That do not leave you alone

Until the end of the eternity,

Until the starting point of the universe,

Until the birth of time.

$\mathcal{Y}$our eyes,

Revealed me.

And I forgot all the words

That with a presentiment

I'd prepared to say.

When your hair

Played amongst my words,

I was thinking of

The incapable words

In turmoil

In front of your eyes,

And of your smile,

Which was not

More than a mere gesture,

But rather an oath,

To burn my lexicons.

*E*verywhere was silent

When you were born.

It was dark

When you smiled

And hearts

Were hardened

When you loved.

The bullet

Passed through your chest

Was dark evil,

Intolerable of

Your smile.

Later,

The darkness remained

In itself,

And gave your eyes

A scream.

*M*y existence,

Entangled

To your existence,

Forms

During a free flow,

Beyond existence

And time.

There will be no blindness,

There will be no death.

My hands will not shake anymore.

It is the time to be

And to speak

Like a child

In your presence,

I've become Jesus with your gaze.

You have the flu,

I guess,

Your throat is inflamed,

Your eyes are watery,

And you have trouble breathing.

Scream

Three times a day,

Gargle happiness before sleep,

Incense your view,

And remember to inject love,

Intramuscularly.

*M*aybe there's still something

That makes life worth living:

Your warm gaze,

Your smile,

Or your kisses.

All are filled with languor,

But your memories

Were rainy

Since the beginning.

*S*ilence!

I hear a cry.

Maybe someone is dead,

Or someone is born.

Maybe someone has left,

Or someone has returned.

Silence!

Maybe someone has fallen in love,

Or someone has lost the love.

Silence!

I hear the wind whispering.

Delighted photons,

Happy photons,

Travelling freely

Through eternity,

From a star in the

Aquarius constellation

To a permanent destination

In your eyes,

In front of mortal kisses

And a finger pointing

Toward a shimmering star

In the infinite space.

We are delighted,

We are happy.

I'm jealous of the air

That embraces you

Fearlessly

And is always with you.

I wish I was the air

That you breathe.

Then I would flow inside you

And transform,

To become you.

*I*t happens

When you don't expect.

A new sight,

And you fall in love again,

As simple as this.

You entered my life,

You left,

As simple as this,

While I was looking

And feeling your kiss.

It will happen again,

Unexpectedly,

As simple as this.

*H*ow come silence

Is the absence of words,

When your eyes

Are crying?

How come life

Stands still

When it's raining?

How come love

Is evitable

When the sunset is wonderful?

How come your love

Is believable

When you're not here?

*B*elieve in the lightness

Of this sound!

The wind is telling

The story of the lawns

For you

And for everyone

Who stands

In parallel lines,

Alert,

And frozen.

Hurry to this sound!

This sound is great.

This sound ends the wars.

This sound whistles in loneliness.

This sound shakes hand with the rain.

This is the sound of the grasses

Under my feet

That were once in love.

When you move

One step away,

The air diffuses

Into my memories,

The flowers become dull,

And my eyes become wet,

Unintentionally.

Go further,

The wind sits tight,

Smokes a cigarette,

And my watch stops working.

Go further still,

More footsteps appear,

Along with shadows other

Than our entangled ones.

And then beyond,

There's a single shadow,

And a single footstep,

And I remember

The wind is not a smoker.

*Y*our gaze

Is a Trojan horse.

It occupies me gradually.

My most incomplete poem

Is the sweetness

Of your kisses.

I can't reach you.

I stay within you.

*T*here's a scent shop

Within me
That sells the scents
Of all women's bodies.

*Y*our presence is a dream

And your absence,

A reality.

You'll distinguish

Love from life
When silence
Is the sole sound.

I'm an amphibian.

I grow up here
And live in your gaze.

*R*eturn my self,

And I'll find a more decent job

Than being a poet.

*T*his is a parallel world:

You are in somebody's arms,
Your memories in mine.

When I walk

With your memories,
There are two pairs of footsteps.
I try to follow yours.

*I*f you are not there,

It doesn't matter

That the most farthest planet has life;

It doesn't have living.

*I*nsomnia is not a disorder.

It's the fear of sleep
And not dreaming about you.

Sometimes your photo smiles:

When it's just me,

My wet eyes,

And simple laws of physics.

*M*y most realistic fiction story is

That someone knocks on the door,

And it's you.

I should've insisted

On you staying.
Then you'd be tenacious enough
To take your memories away too.

*T*he Jazz piano

Makes me come alive,

And kills again

With every note.

Similar to your kisses.

*T*here's always time

For farewells.

Let something remains forever.

$\mathcal{B}$e my panacea

With every kiss

When I die of your last kiss.

A secret is locked on

Your lips.
It'll be opened
By kissing.

*L*eave the mirror

With your finger-print
And lip-print on it.
I want my kiss every morning.

"Close your eyes,"

You said.

"So I don't fall into your gaze."

I did,

And fell into your breath

Instead.

S ometimes,

Something

Is too far away,

Even a hopeful mind

Can't reach to it.

*T*he lights are out,

Or you shut your eyes,

To the smile

I drew on the wall.

$\mathcal{B}$e God

And create kisses

On my lips.

I'll be Satan

If I don't worship you.

I am drunk

When your hair
Is burgundy
And your lips
Are red.

I designed clothes

For shadows

From your gaze.

Nobody can distinguish

Their shadows

From stones

Anymore.

*H*is stare at the broken mirror

Reveals her

In the fragments of images

Of his eyes,

That are waiting for her.

I'm jealous of the words

That hold you naked,

That impregnate you.

You'll give birth

To me,

A poet.

*Y*our gaze

Like the monsoon rains,

Pours upon me,

Then you look away

And leave me

With flooded eyes.

I had a feverish dream,

I guess,

The night you kissed my forehead.

I'd never seen the moon

That close.

When you call me

By my name,

I won't get lost

Among all the air molecules

That line up

To kiss your lips.

I'm addicted to

The vineyard

Of your body,

And the wine

Of your lips.

Be my oldest wine,

And I'll be drunk

Every night.

*T*here's an emptiness

Inside me.

When you look,

It's not there;

When you don't,

It is.

I'm an Alien

From the space of your lips.

*T*he leaves

Can't endure

The winter

In your absence.

They fall at your foot,

Begging you to stay.

On the grooves of sidewalks,

There are traces

Of the kisses,

Of those lips

That are now traces

On the grooves of sidewalks.

*W*hen you come,

Don't bring your painting colors,

I won't have words either.

Your presence alone

Is painting

And poetry.

I'm snow

In your embrace.
It warms me up,
Melts me down,
Kills me.

*Y*our presence

Is a spring afternoon
Under the sunlight,
And your absence
Is an early autumn.

*I*f I continue to be

A poet,

Who will deal with

This persistent gloominess

If you don't stay.

After each period

A sentence awaits,
Like all the dots
You left in my memories.

I waited for the rain

To look back at you,

When you waved goodbye.

My eyes seemed

Wet from the rain.

What should I do

With your eyes:
Die in them?
Then you'd bring me back to life
With your gaze.
Or be born in them
And fall in love with your breaths?
What if I'm not in the air you breathe?

*U*pon your shoulders,

Plants grow

From my kisses,

And they blossom

Upon your breasts

Flowers that only bloom

In the island of your embrace,

The island made of you,

And me,

And the wine of your eyes.

I'm a pawn

In your chess game.
I'll either die,
Or leave the game.

*M*y heart

Nags like a tired baby

For you.

And I'm the darkness

Of a room

That doesn't let it sleep.

*Y*ou don't change

Your clothes,

Your lipstick,

And your perfume

When you return to my mind.

*W*hen you read poetry,

Words turn into butterflies

And rest on your lips.

Then,

I'm a worried

Butterfly hunter.

A statue,

Without mouth and ears,

On top of the most highest

Mountain of stupidity,

Tries desperately,

Again and again,

To prove love

To earthworms

Of a distant island.

*C*lose your eyes,

Then I'll hide in

Your arms,

Your hair,

Your gaze.

Then you attempt to find me,

For eternity.

*S*catter everything!

Put the sky on the library shelves,

Put the trees between the pages

Of books,

And tie the earth

To the dandelions.

No! Your lips stay

Where they are.

*C*ould I stare at the mirror

And see you?

Could I touch my face

And it's yours?

Could I think about you

And you knock on the door?

Could I read poetry

And you reply: yes my dear?

Oh my gray muse!

*S*creams

That harden on the walls

Will become machetes

That cut your throat.

Remember the screams;

The walls will fall.

The candle

We made to help us see

Will melt down

On the eyes of an opaque image

Of you and me and our shadows

When nobody cares to look.

*T*he splinters of stars,

The fragments of earth,

And the drops of rain,

Are words of my silence

When I look at your eyes.

When it starts,

I end.

When it finishes,

I begin.

This is how I write poetry

About you.

Shall I ask the sky

To shower you?
So the desert,
The thorn bush,
The silence,
And I without you,
Get drunk.

You said: say blue!

I said: you!

You said: say green!

I said: you!

You said: say red!

I said: you!

This is how I write poetry,

And how you paint.

*T*his is pure madness:

Without you,

I became the shadow

Of your shadow,

And the taste of your kisses.

While without me,

You became anything and everything.

$\mathcal{A}$ single crow

Is sufficient

For autumn days,

And my gaze

For your footsteps,

To break the silence

Of a hopeless alley.

Your lips are goldfish

Surrounded by a bowl

Of my memories.

Sometimes they kiss the shell,

Sometimes they surface to breathe,

And one morning they'll die.

*F*rozen lights,

Dull voices,

And abandoned loves,

Are in the luggage of those

Who live somewhere,

And left their hearts

Elsewhere .

*M*y excuses

Are colorless.

Embrace them easily,

Kiss them,

Breathe them,

So they turn green

Red and blue.

Oh you

My two-colored eye muse!

I'm fire,

You're smoke.

When I start,

You begin.

When I sink down,

You rise up.

And there's always a kissing distance

Between us.

I swear to your two-colored eyes.

I said: mom,

Your hands smell like heaven.

She said: because I patted your head.

I said: Your gaze warms me up.

She said: because I looked at you.

I said: how about your face wrinkles?

She said: they are the distances

Between me and you.

*T*he traces of your gaze

Sometimes come out

Like fossils,

And I'm like an archeologist

Who can neither cover you,

Nor discover you.

$y$our distance

Is a bird

Whose talons are in my eyes,

And whose wings are on my shoulders.

It lays seeds inside my brain

Of a plant

That roots when you come,

And dries when you kiss me.

*O*ne morning when I wake up,

I ask all the women

To place flowers on your hair.

This way, your photo

Looks more beautiful,

And the room smells

Like you.

*S*imply you come,

Simply you look at me,

Simply you kiss me,

Simply you leave.

Then I'm alone

With a simple embrace.

Such is my simple life.

"Wine or kisses?", you asked,

And I was stoned with your gaze.
"Gaze or embrace?", you asked,
And I was drowning in your arms,
"You or I?", you asked,
And I was you.

*Y*our long hair

Covers your breasts

And swings like two beautiful,

Venomous snakes.

I long to kiss them;

They long to

Eat my brain.

Your love

Wasn't what you brought

One day,

And took away

Another day.

Your love

Stayed on the walls,

On the gramophone,

And on the old books.

You brought yourself,

And took me away.

*I*ndifference

Is a fruit

That grows from

The wrinkles of your eyelids,

And has the taste of

Your heartbeat.

A fruit

That has seeds

In your hatred,

And roots

In your cold hands

That one day swirl around

Your neck.

Be different!

*P*aint a red fairy

For me

On the shores of Normandy.

I remain silent

And become a poppy

Under your brushstrokes.

When you are not here,

I get consumed

With the taste of wet boots,

And nauseating embraces.

Stay!

When you come here,

Wear perfume of your body's scent,

A cloth of your skin,

A lipstick of your lips,

Earrings of your ears,

And a necklace of your breasts.

It's cold in here.

You have to have enough clothing.

*T*his is not a dream.

You suddenly appear,

Sit in front of me,

Kiss me,

And when I turn my head,

You disappear.

This is not a dream.

This is the reverse reality.

*I*n my dream,

Two birds

Were entangled together

On your shoulders,

And two kisses

On my lips.

When I woke up,

There was a vulture

Over my bed,

And some kisses

On the window.

*N*either your smile,

Nor your kisses,

Nor your embrace,

Distinguish you

From other women.

It's the memory

Of you leaving

That stayed,

And doesn't go away.

*I*t's surprising

If you come over,
Sit in front of me
And throw an apple upward.
Then I stare at your feet
That didn't come.

*T*his graveyard

Is sufficient

To destroy all the moments.

I'm crucified

To this ticking sound of the clock,

To this look,

To this snow

Outside the window,

And to this kiss marks

On your fingerprints

On the window.

I'm cold,

Therefore I am.

I pin your scent

To the shadows of women.

When you are absent,

Their shadows rise,

Embrace me,

And leave.

Then I'm alone

With pins in my body.

*L*ove is silent

When you say, "I love you".
And it's silent
When you look into her eyes
And say nothing.
Love was born mute,
And will die mute.

Someday the streets

Chase the dreams of you.

Then the city is empty

With no roads,

No pavement,

No rain.

It'll be just me

And the memory of our walk.

The best long-lasting gift

You ever receive

Is the poetry you hear

Every year

From other men

Holding flowers,

Demanding your kisses,

And reading my words to you.

Those words

That originated from your body,

And terminate on it again.

*Y*our voice

Gradually changes into

A lyric,

And invades

The empty spaces

Between my words,

The inaccessible silence

Made of you and me,

And lots of mute memories.

My poetry is now

A symphony

Of silent notes.

$y$our embrace

Is my shelter,

And your breasts

Shine like two suns.

Braid your hair

Like a rope

To tie my hands,

And kiss me,

Like a moment,

To convince me to stay.

*O*ne day

You wake up,

And taste my kisses

On your lips,

As much as there was a distance

Between us,

Greater than your breath,

From the beginning of the world

To the end.

I swear to your immortality,

And your cheek dimple.

My arms will die.

I'll not be able

To look into your eyes.

From this distant silent man,

Ashes will remain

That make the wind

Fall in love,

Blow in your hair,

And embrace you

On the beach that was calling us.

*T*here's only a constant noise

Remaining from your voice.

When I drown myself,

The noise fades away gradually

And I become free.

When they pull me out,

There's neither your voice,

Nor your cold hands,

Nor that fucking annoying noise.

*P*assing through

A checkerboard pattern

Of a parallel dream

And ups and downs

Of me and you

And the glimmers

Of the interrupted words,

We reached to the rain

(Without umbrellas)

We conceived by

The stripped moments,

And by the never-arriving seconds.

As such begins

The life of an amphibious creature.

$\mathcal{D}$on't trust my words.

Take them,

And taste them,

And seed your gaze

In my mouth,

Like a plant that roots

Inside me,

And blooms thorns

In my brain,

And its fruits pours out

Of my mouth,

Like a poem about you.

When you raise your head,

I rise to the sky,

So that I may fall

With the rain,

On your cheeks,

Your breasts,

So that I may roll

In your embrace,

And return to earth again.

Oh my tallest muse,

Look at the moon.

What pass by

Are the shadows

Of my worry

On the shoulders of moments

That overflow

Into memories of you,

Somewhere between

A regret for the time

You closed your eyes,

And when time stopped.

I am now used to

The game of shadows.

*T*he world comes to an end tonight,

Somewhere very close,

Closer than you,

And farther than

The scattered,

Parallel,

Temporary,

Universes.

The world comes to an end tonight,

Among the smoke and wine,

The tasteless kisses,

And the indifference to the silence

Of rooms.

The world comes to an end tonight,

To the world of tomorrow.

We can't hear

A woman who closes her eyes,

And digs her fingernails

Into her palms,

Meaning the earth is round,

And her legs

Fractured by gravity,

And her body,

In violation of

The Laws of Thermodynamics,

Is colder than earth,

And man.

We can't hear

The woman who has broken

The sound barrier.

When it comes to migration,

Waters freeze,

And three kisses

Remain on the window.

Along with daily stereotypes

Only your eyes are wet,

As are my shoulders.

I have experienced

The return,

And I know you didn't live

All the moments,

I have experienced

The leaving,

And I know I didn't live.

I was wandering among

The seasons,

And I was thinking about

Wind and rain,

Unaware of your whisper

In my ears.

I looked at the sky,

I saw your smile,

Then I walked through a season

That has flowers of your smile,

The warmth of your embrace,

The leaves mixed in your hair,

And when you are absent,

It's cold.

*L*ook! I said,

The sand suits my hands,

And the water suits your eyes.

Look! you said,

The sea is our distance,

And the shore is your shoulders.

Look! I said,

The bird is my love,

And the fish is your unattainability.

Look! you said,

The kiss suits my lips,

And the silence suits yours.

My territory is where

Your name grows out of the trees,

The winds bring your scent,

The sun has the warmth of

Your embrace,

And you glow at nights.

I'm Mahyar the First.

This is my territory,

And you are its protective Ahura.

$\mathcal{A}$ mere breath has left

From a memory

That kisses your neck,

And from the drops,

That drip on your breasts.

I breeze over your body

Like a bird

In love with a distant fish,

And with every dive,

It neither dies

Nor becomes alive.

[to 2009 Iranian Green Movement leaders]

*T*he old bricks

Scream.

The cold bars

Bleed.

And freedom

Stays quiet

At a dead end alley.

The men's eyes

Are worried;

A woman's,

Sad.

Yet another man is insane

On a sand throne.

There'll be a storm.

Someday I rush into your gaze,

And from your books,

The newspapers across your room,

The notes of songs you play,

The paintings on the wall,

Your coffee cup,

The air molecules,

I enter your eyes,

Then your blood,

And flow in your entire body.

Then you have no place to escape.

*T*here's an inanity

In each second

That impels me to your absence.

That's a secret

Between me

And your memories.

*Y*our memories

Invade my mind

Like whales

That die on a shore.

Without you,

My breaths form an airy shape
Of you
That stays forever.

Where on our way

I lost you,

That I hear your footsteps

Approaching.

But you're years away.

$\mathcal{L}$eaving,

Requires bold and hopeless steps.
Though I have hope for steps
To come.

*E*nd of story

Is a temptation

Of having your memories,

Or the memory of having you.

This is my share of your

To be or not to be.

*T*he seconds were lucky

To count your breaths

And heartbeats.

The years weren't.

$\mathcal{U}$pon the branches

Shaken down by the wind,

A bird's dream

Tolerates flying.

A bird

In love with

The last leaf,

That will be freed

By the storm.

*Y*our hands,

Similar to the sun,

Are dominating

The darkness of a land.

Not to mention my destiny

That will be dark

In your hair.

Since sometime,

Something is not the same
Between you and me.
Since you left without me,
And I stayed with you.

[To my friend who died young]

*I*n everlasting turbulence,

Are the roots of a tree
That dried in the spring,
And the dreams of the garden
Bloomed on its branches,
Somewhere between the earth
And the sky.

A bird was suturing

Sticks

To the gloomy sky.

So maybe the spring

Lays eggs in its nest,

And at the end of autumn,

It can count its fears

That are ready to swallow

The earth's pains.

*I*f the snow

Falls slower,

My footprints

Melt

And drip

On the flickers

Of a light

That lived

To see the spring.

*T*he end of the story

Is a resonance

Of the vibration of your lips

With the air

That condenses

On the closed windows,

And the words

That flow under your fingertips,

That writes something carelessly,

While the moisture

Cries.

The end of the resonance

Is my mind

Without your thoughts.

*L*et this poem remains romantic!

Don't knock on the door,

Don't open the windows,

Don't tie the flowers to your hair,

Don't look at me,

Don't be

In my thoughts.

Let this poem remains romantic!

*I*f there was enough strength,

It would be possible to talk about you

So much

That all voices

Would become wounded,

And their blood,

Would carve a line in front of you.

Alas! You pressed your feet firmly

On the throats of words,

And you sent them

To fight your gaze,

That made silence public.

Scattered pieces,

A hollow skull,
Empty orbits,
And anxious phalanges,
Over your body.
I was amongst the pieces,
Looking for that moment
You dried up in me,
And I became a piece

In your heart.

This was the beginning

Of when the wind

Resonated in the skull,

And it sounded like

You leaving.

When it rained,

My orbit filled with water,

And the wet termites

Were in love.

*T*he sun will return one day,

And ask, "Where are your eyes?"

And you were thinking

That the end of this darkness

Is the return of the sun;

Therefore,

You put your eyes

On the way,

For the lost steps,

And bound your hands

On the broken branches

Of the wind.

This time everybody will return,

And they find the sun

In your eyes.

*F*ear

Is a man,

Entrapped

In the sound of footsteps

In the street,

And bravery

Is a woman,

Passing the street

And thinking about

The man's freedom.

$\mathcal{A}$t night

When you start your enchantments,

I run

And sit far away

To watch you,

Frightened and bewildered.

Your banality

Isn't out of life,

And your lust

Isn't out of need.

At night

When you wipe the dust

From rainbows,

I sit far away

To watch the lust of life,

Frightened and bewildered.

Your loneliness

Isn't out of death,

And your desire

Isn't out of whim.

At night

When you undress,

I sit far away

And watch the whim of death.

$\mathcal{N}$ot by a transient dream

Of an everlasting love,

But by a transient wake

Of your presence,

Or by a weak whisper

Of your words,

The mortal moments

Are being pleased.

*T*he smell of gunpowder

Is the scent of a woman

In love with

An enemy soldier,

And dies with every shot.

A shelter

Is a woman,

Waiting.

Destruction

Is a woman,

Worried,

And silent.

Dismiss all the soldiers.

Let the women make love.

The world will be better.

Spread on the wings

Of a phoenix,

Ashes from a necklace

Of the pearls

Once worn around a neck.

What shall rise from the ashes?

A plant

Or a destructive fire?

Hey! The phoenix should have a match

Who has the elixir

To transmute the ashes

Into the pearls.

$\mathcal{U}$pon the shoulders

Of destiny,

A God is crying

Whose providence is

To be born

From whores,

Whose fate

Produces divinity.

Alas!

Satan is the twin

Who is born,

And swallows the mother.

*T*he seconds

Are different:
One welcomes you
Early;
One returns late
From your dream,
And one sits back
And stares at a clock

Missing hands that you took.

I'm at the fourth second though.

*H*ow many trains

Were like this?
Not whistling,
And not breaking your heart
When they left.
The stations
Cried spontaneously
For the luggage

Left behind,

And for the hands

Not waving goodbye.

Something had begun

For those who left,

And something was ending

For those who stayed.

Only the world of luggage

Left behind

Had neither any beginning,

Nor any ending.

*L*ook,

The vase is also missing you,

And dries the roots,

Not to mention my feet.

I told you to sing,

I told you to whisper,

I told you to be quiet,

Didn't I?

Wasn't it enough;

The stories we read,

And increased

Our anxiety?

Wasn't it enough;

Those efforts,

That even made the sun

Dark and night?

One thousand and one nights,

And at the dawn of

A thousand and two,

It fell asleep with your kiss

And never awakened.

This is the fate of

Rotten roots,

Oh my beautiful flower!

*I*t all started from your hands,

From your palms indeed.

That day your palm was hot,

And I felt

Something was about to happen.

My fingertips burned

On your palm

As if an army

Invaded my head

From your palm

Through my fingers,

An army of knights

Longing for your kisses.

My head was a throne for a queen,

Dreaming about

Her baby becoming the King.

It all ended with your hands though,

On a winter's night

When a dead baby was born,

And your hands were around its neck.

$\mathcal{Y}$our husband

Was admiring your cooking skills,
And I was thinking
About my raw hands,
Burnt around your body.

*T*he unwritten words

Pull the story swamp

Down to watch,

And the narrator

Down to wisdom.

*M*y words

Do not consent

To write about you

When they are satisfied

With your absence.

$\mathcal{A}$ child is playing around

Inside me,

Asking for you.

Neither my poetry,

Nor my lullaby

Calms it down.

Come back and be a mother.

*I*f we were pleased

With rain,
Random drippings
Were kind of a test
For our patience,
And kind of pleasure
For your return
In rain.

*T*he universe was warmer

At the beginning,

And our dust specks were close.

Don't worry!

This separation is not your fault;

The universe is close to its end.

*O*ne could laugh

With your mouth,
One could feel
With your hands,
One could see
With your eyes,
One could beat
With your heart,

One could reach you

With your feet.

One could love you

With you.

When I pass the sidewalk,

There are lots of dating places
Under my feet.
In each, the wind is blowing,
And a kiss is still waiting
To sit on some lips.

I knit kisses

On your body,

To lay in your arms

During the winter.

When the spring arrives,

Your pullover

Is a rootland of me

That you take out.

*T*he translation of all words

Are some silent syllables

That stand in front of you.

When you look at them,

They become alive

And turn into poetry.

You are a poet in all languages.

*T*here should be a territory

To live in,

Where the laws are

Some poems about you.

Then everyone would obey

Your eyes,

The crosswalks,

Yield to your words.

At night, there's a blackout

In your hair.

Days start

With your voice,

And election

Is wanting you.

You should be the final word,

And I'd become a censored newspaper

In your arms.

This is the sole democratic-dictatorship

Of the world.

*A*t sunset,

The shadows of my fingers

Flow down the wall

On the piano keys,

The blood coagulates

In the note's throat,

And the waiting

Adjusts its seat.

The shadows crawl over

Each octave,

And a distance falls between

You and my fingertips.

At night

My fingertips penetrate into

Your body,

And the waiting

Plays a silent symphony.

When the words settle down,

The loneliness,

Like a woman with disturbed hair,

Undresses in front of me,

Embraces me,

Puts her tongue in my mouth,

And plants the seed of words

In my throat.

I run my hand through her hair;

It becomes running sand,

And her tongue

Flames out of my chest.

The words,

Like cursed babies,

Spray out into air,

And the wall

Becomes a draft of your dreams.

I look for L, I

You look for P,

Then we put them together

To make silence.

*E*verything should make us

Be a poet:
Anything we touch,
Anything we watch,
Any word,
Any sound,
Any color,
Any continuous honking of cars
In traffic,

Any light that shimmers,

Any book that is unread,

Any date finished forever,

Any love frozen in hearts,

Any fraud,

Any presence at religious sites,

Any rubbery,

Any dictatorship,

Any kid throwing a stone at tanks,

Any missile that kills mothers,

Should make everyone a poet.

Because poetry is the only

Salve for life.

Because poetry is the only

Antidote.

When they cut the trees,

Picked up the flowers,

Toxified the water,

And polluted the air,

Nothing remained to be done.

So they ripped off

Each other

To lay back in their private gardens,

Breathe the fresh air deeply,

Drink beer,

While watching-with hesitation-

The news of floods,

Avalanches,

Tornados,

Hungers,

And poverties.

Then they look for their iPhone

Using their iWatch,

Call their partner

In the Middle East

To reassure them

The soldiers eat organic foods,

To fight against terrorism,

Healthy.

It's hard work,

They have to remember

To attend

The memorial in solidarity with

The recent terror attacks.

*I*s it possible to hold everything

In a memory?

Is it possible to trust memory?

That doesn't change something,

Doesn't bind our pictures together,

Doesn't braid your hair with my hands,

Doesn't make fresh coffee,

Doesn't bring you back,

Sitting in front of me,

Looking at me,

Penetrating my memories.

Is it possible?

The memory is not

Trustworthy,

Oh my far dream,

Come and protect my memories.

When we were walking in the park,

Your hands like a compass

Pointed to the playing kids,

And out from your fingertips,

Our children

Entered into the dreams

Of a swing

That stared at the sky,

Awaiting rain.

Oh my rain!

How did you pour over

The children's games

That your fingers dried,

And that no swing

Could elevate the children of sky,

Anymore.

Oh my raincoat!

How did you get wet

On my body,

When kisses poured off the sky,

And our share

Was given to the goldfish

In the park pool.

Oh my umbrella!

How did you become a base

For showering those

Who looked like you,

But no one would let them

Play water games.

Oh my rainy day!

Pour,

That in stormy days

The park is closed,

And I could sit at home all day

And watch you

And your children

From the window.

My head is a rootland.

I'm a plant

Where my feet grow down

To the ground,

And from the other side,

They come out,

Bloom

And pollinate.

Your seasonal allergies

Are my chronic foot pain,

When every spring

My feet bloom

And your eyes get wet.

Humidity is bad for aching feet,

And dry weather

For roots.

We should find a solution

For climate change,

And bring together

Two points of earth.

I'll stay away

Someday,

From those vague sounds

That fill the shapeless void

Of your presence.

I'll understand again

The meaning of those heavy moments

That pass by a man

On a bridge

Waiting to jump.

I'll be an expectant shrine,

That a woman offers her existence

To,

Recklessly.

I'll be a stranger

Among those kisses

That never happened.

I'll become you

Someday.

$\mathcal{T}$he day you returned,

It was raining fish,

The butterflies flew towards

The Arctic,

And the elephants

Put their ears on the ground,

To predict your arrival.

The day you returned,

It was night,

And I was waiting for you.

*T*hose words of a poem

About you,

Came to take you away,

But they left your pieces

Inside me.

Now those pieces

And the negligent everydayness

Are heavy,

And the words try vigorously,

That your corpse

Doesn't stink.

$\mathcal{B}$e my seasons

And my calendar,

With no significant event.

Be my winter clothing,

My spring raincoat

And umbrella,

Wettable.

Be my summer fruits,

Unripe.

Be my autumn leaves,

Mute.

Be my plantable grass,

Swirl around my body,

Poisonous.

Be my everydayness,

And my occasional excitement.

Be my birthday,

And my moment of death.

Be a jump in my dream,

Down to a valley,

That reaches to your hair

On a shore.

Be the awakeness at midnight

Because of the numb arm.

Be the wind whistle,

From the window seam.

Be an empty space

On the bed.

Be the sentence, "I miss you",

Told to the silent breath

On the other side of the phone,

Be long syllables

Among the empty spaces of poetry.

Be me,

When I say, "I love you".

*T*he rain is sorrowful

For the cloud,

Mourning in exile

From the earth.

Every spring

The droplets turn into

Melancholic pearls,

Upon sliding down

A woman's black hair.

At winter

They turn into

The shimmering glitters

Of heavenly Esfandiar,

In exile,

Hoping those disconsolate eyes

Bloom again,

In exile.

If it rains,

The smell of the soil

Will distress the cloud again.

*T*ime flows elegantly

Under your feet,
And finds itself
In busy cafés,
At different decades,
Where men constantly
Fell in love with you,
And you

Carelessly

Disperse your hair

In the wind,

Therefore every inhalation

Of air

Rose with excitement

And held with longing.

The streets

Became light

Of aimless passage

Of loveless people,

When you once pass them.

The shops spread

Their charm

To your eyes

That light up

Once they look at those

Agitated wishful men.

This scene will be filmed

Thousands of times,

And I'll be the actor

Sitting at the corner

Of the café,

In love with you,

And before I meet you,

There will be a cut command.

All the pathways are the same,

And as time goes by,

They become filled

With a feeling

More than they can tolerate.

You could stand at a corner

And watch the end of the path

That flows empty

In the memories of

Those who passed it.

Every person

Has its own pathway,

Who carries around

Everywhere

And sets it up,

And suddenly all the noises

Of people,

All the scents and smokes

Of cafés,

The dampness in the air,

And the color of melancholy,

Are the same as what they were.

That is how all the pathways

Are the same,

When you carry around

Your melancholia

Everywhere.

Life is an austerity,

And it counts down

Mathematically.

Numbers are being born,

Being raised.

Even numbers,

Odd numbers,

Unemployed numbers,

Street numbers with many zeros

Following them,

Numbers that explode,

Fall down,

Be shot,

And become the title of

The mainstream media.

Prime numbers,

Numbers with absolute values

Larger than them.

We are number sequences,

That live mathematically

A life of austerity,

So that statistics

Remain an authentic science.

*E*mpty bubbles,

Thin colorful bubbles,

Dancing bubbles

In the wind,

Bubbles that grow

Rise

And burst,

The same as a kid

With an illusion of being an adult

That let go of the mother's hand.

Running, is a way of escaping.

Nobody will be suspicious

Of who is standing still.

Standing doesn't disorder

The arrangement of the trees.

Running is a threshold

For freedom.

There's always something

Far from us,

Even when it's too close.

How could you run into

The solitude of a human

That has no other way

Than staying and waiting?

How could you trust

Long ordered lineups?

When,

Not achieving,

Is a common song

Between the solitude of humans

And the incidents,

That restlessly run away and far,

The same as the colorful bubbles

In the children's games.

How could you show an escape plan

To those indifferent bubbles

That are waiting to be born,

So they don't end up bursting?

Thin dancing bubbles,

Children's happiness in a normal day,

And the mother holds the kid's hand

Again,

Among the indifferent loud crowd.

*L*ove was a simple word

Flowing on tongues,

But mouths were filled

With dark soil,

And the hearts were

More worthless

Than a phoenix cage.

Upon a mouth

That was disclosing love,

A kiss

Was laying eggs

Like a pigeon

Waiting for life to be born,

And kindness was growing

Out of a wall crack.

We took the flesh

As love

And like a scarecrow

On a sand throne,

Watched the crows parade.

Oh, I wish love

Was only a simple word,

Flowing on tongues,

Oh, I wish kindness

Was growing on the wall.

$\mathcal{M}$elancholia

Is like a soldier who

Marches on a muddy battlefield

Forward and downward,

And is buried more and more

With every step

Until fully concealed,

And nobody realizes the soldier

Is still marching underground,

The same as the melancholia

That penetrates bones.

*D*eath is everything,

And is none.

Death is a school

Ruined by alphabets,

To force the kids' dreams

To become educated.

Death is the shadow of a tree

Over the flight of a tired bird.

Death is the sound of your footsteps

When you go away.

Death is a traffic light

That counts the heartbeats of

Child street workers.

Death is becoming numb

In the scent of your hair,

Maniac,

Lost.

Death is the only thing left for a woman

In the entire world

When her child is executed,

Innocent.

Death is the pain,

Silent in Khavaran.

Death is the look of a mother

Seeing a soldier's tag and some bones.

Death is the sole speaker

Among the fearful tongues.

Death is a memory in sleep.

Death is a father's embrace

Under the broken house.

Death is a question mark

In front of lots of exclamation marks.

Death is the memory of you running

In the memory of me looking.

Death is a dream in life.

Death is a dreamy life.

*T*here's still some hope left.

Don't be sad, oh my rain,

The sky still becomes gloomy

And searches for you.

Don't be sad, oh my shelter,

This roof,

For thousands of years,

Has tolerated

Storm,

Dust,

Invasion of Mongols,

The battle of Chaldiran,

The bombing of Hiroshima,

The war in Normandy,

And Aleppo.

Don't be sad my spring blossom.

Do you hear?

The crows of the third millennium

Before Christ

Also waited for some footsteps

During autumn,

That could break the silence of alleys.

All the sounds remain

In the atmosphere.

We are surrounded by

All the speeches, fights, sounds

Forever.

We are surrounded by the screams

Of dinosaurs,

The sound of lashes

On Jesus' body,

The sound of lovemaking,

Of Mohammad.

The sound of

Centuries of silence,

The sound of the gunfire

To Abbas Mirza,

Surrounded by the screams of battles,

The pains of rapes.

We are all surrounded by

The screams of earth.

Don't be sad, Oh my rebuilding,

There's still a way

To recreate this tuneless instrument.

You can still hold someone's hand

And grow a plant on it.

There's still a way

To not be punished.

There's still some hope,

Oh my hope.

About the Author

Mahyar Mazloumi, is an Iranian-Canadian poet and writer. He was born in 1981 in Iran and immigrated to Canada in 2009 to receive his PhD in Nanotechnology. For him science and poetry share the same root: imagination. He started to write modern Persian poetry when he was 17. Since then he has been involved in lots of poetry groups and programs and has won a few awards in short story and poetry such as the JUDGE'S CHOICE AWARDS for the 2017 Ultra Short Poem Competition of The Ontario Poetry Society and 2009 Loh's short story competition in Iran. He is also passionate about photography and painting. He won the runner up award for the 2018 Doors Open Ottawa photography competition. In 2016-2017 he hosted a show about Persian poetry at the Ottawa Iranian radio "Namashoom". You can follow him on Instagram @mahyarmaz

18818734R00168

Made in the USA
Middletown, DE
02 December 2018